JANE ADDAMS

by Jacquelyn Mitchard

For a free color catalog describing Gareth Stevens' list of high-quality children's books, call 1-800-341-3569 (USA) or 1-800-461-9120 (Canada).

Picture Credits

The Bettmann Archive — 12 (below), 17, 19, 22, 23, 26, 28, 36, 38, 41, 42, 44, 45, 46, 50, 54, 55, 57; map by Sharon Burris, © Gareth Stevens, Inc., 1990 — 60; The Corcoran Gallery of Art — 6, 12 (above); Lake County Museum, Curt Teich Postcard Archives, Wauconda, Illinois — 25, 30 (both), 37, 52; Harry J. Quinn, © 1990 — cover; University of Hartford: Museum of American Political Life — 43; University of Illinois at Chicago, University Library, Jane Addams Memorial Collection — 4, 6 (both), 9 (both), 10, 15, 16, 18, 24, 30, 32, 33, 34, 35, 48, 56, 59; UPI/Bettmann — 29.

Cover: In this drawing, Jane Addams stands before a modern-day banner promoting peace.

A Gareth Stevens Children's Books edition

Edited, designed, and produced by
Gareth Stevens Children's Books
1555 North RiverCenter Drive, Suite 201
Milwaukee, Wisconsin 53212, USA

Library of Congress Cataloging-in-Publication Data

Mitchard, Jacquelyn.
    Jane Addams / by Jacquelyn Mitchard.
       p. cm. — (People who have helped the world)
    Summary: A biography of the social worker who promoted world peace and neighborhood cooperation.
    ISBN 0-8368-0144-X
    1. Addams, Jane 1860-1935—Juvenile literature. 2. Social workers—United States—Biography—Juvenile literature. 3. Women social reformers—United States—Biography—Juvenile literature. 4. Addams, Jane 1860-1935. [1. Social workers.] I. Title. II. Series.
    HV40.32.A33M58   1990   361.92—dc20   [B]   [92]   89-49624

Series conceived by Helen Exley
Series editor: Amy Bauman
Editorial assistants: Scott Enk, Diane Laska, John D. Rateliff, Jennifer Thelen
Picture researcher: Daniel Helminak
Layout: Kristi Ludwig

Printed in the United States of America

1 2 3 4 5 6 7 8 9 95 94 93 92 91

JANE ADDAMS

Pioneer in social reform and activist for world peace

by Jacquelyn Mitchard

Gareth Stevens Children's Books
MILWAUKEE

Life in the city

Night had stilled the slum streets of Chicago's Near West Side.

But not everyone was asleep. In the 1890s, this corner of the teeming city never slept entirely. A rag man walked with his cart through the mud, his weary horse clomping along beside him. From far off came a volley of shouts as exhausted factory workers, their frustration fueled by an evening at the local saloon, turned on one another with their fists. A sick baby awoke and cried out weakly. But these sounds of the night were the sounds of peace for the many thousands of foreign-born residents who lived here crushed together in shacks, frame houses, and cheap apartments. They slept deeply, unhearing.

During the day, these same streets roared with life. Dirty children played in the mud and manure that was everywhere. Little boys, tough beyond their years, turned hard eyes on weaker playmates, hoping to snatch away the few pennies that some trusting mother had given her child to buy food at the street market. These streets were a dangerous place both day and night. In this new land, poverty had ground many immigrants' dreams of prosperity to dust. It sometimes made even good people desperate.

Building a legend

This night, a young woman slept in an upper bedroom in one of the few "nice" houses left standing in the neighborhood. Although the old red brick house may have looked fine to nearby slum dwellers, it was a soot-covered, sagging memory of its original self. The young woman, worn out after her long day, turned in her bed and then woke with a start. Someone or something was in the room with her.

Opposite: At twenty-eight, Jane Addams knew she wanted to use her life to serve humanity but wasn't sure how. She grew deeply troubled that her high moral principles weren't being set to action and were therefore useless. It was a theme she would stress all her life.

New immigrants waiting for clearance to enter the United States are captured in the painting In the Land of Promise *by artist Charles Ulrich.*

Then she saw the intruder: a man crouched in the shadows at the end of her bed. Gruffly, he demanded money. The woman sat up in bed, curious. "Why do you want it?" she asked without a trace of fear.

"I'm hungry," the man muttered, "and I can't find a job."

"All right," the woman answered. "The money is in the top drawer, over there. But if you really want a job, come back here tomorrow." The man took the money and slipped away without another word. But the next day, he did come back. The young woman was not surprised. She knew that people's basic good natures often overcame their worst impulses. She kept her promise and helped the man who had robbed her find a job. He eventually repaid the money he had stolen.

The young woman was Jane Addams. The story of the robber in the night was just one of the stories that people loved to tell about her and the forty-six years that she spent in the big brick house called Hull House. Hull House was one of the first settlement houses to serve the poor immigrant families who came to Chicago at the dawn of America's industrial revolution. This institution helped many generations of people rise out of lives of brutal poverty.

A social worker ahead of her time

In later years, Addams was often called upon to speak about founding Hull House. When she spoke, she never cast herself in the role of heroine. As *Life* magazine photographer Wallace Kirkland, who lived and worked at Hull House for nearly fifteen years, said, "She didn't care who got the credit — just so the thing was done." Addams simply was not interested in fame. Even in her biographical listing in *Who's Who*, she ignored some of her many honors and accomplishments to proudly list "garbage inspector" among her occupations. She had truly held that job for a time in Chicago's Nineteenth Ward — the area in which Hull House was located — and was proud of that fact.

Although she would not admit it, Jane Addams was a genius. She was a far-sighted social worker even before that term existed. Through her work, she pioneered a new way to help poor people — a way that became the model for today's social work. Addams' method was simple. She had realized early on that poor people needed more than charity. They needed dignity. And dignity, she saw, did not come from handouts given at arm's length. It came from a hand extended in understanding. Most of all, Jane Addams knew that if a nation's poorest people are left to suffer, their needs eat away at the quality of everyone's lives.

Jane Addams discovered Hull House in 1889. She looked beneath the decades of dirt and saw the building's beauty.

In the 1800s, immigrant parents often worked long hours, leaving their children alone all day. For this reason, Hull House's day-care center, kindergarten, and open kitchen were well received in the neighborhood.

In her time, Jane Addams became one of the most outstanding women in the United States. Wherever she went, people turned out in droves to meet her. Some of the wealthiest and most powerful of these people competed to support her work. Her visits to other countries often resembled royal tours. Even presidents sought her opinion. In 1931, she received the Nobel Prize for her work toward world peace. As Professor Frederick Stang of the Nobel Committee presented the award to her, he called her "America's uncrowned queen." And later, another observer called her "the only saint America has produced."

Jane Addams' people

But the regard of the people was Addams' greatest reward. She would have been moved, had she seen them, by the grief-stricken faces of the people who came to Hull House when she died on May 21, 1935. That day, people began filing in to pay their respects at dawn and continued in vast numbers all day long. Sometimes as many as two thousand people an hour crowded the house, the line extending through the courtyard and down the street.

Politicians, police officers, and peddlers came. Workmen came before their factory shifts began, setting down their lunch buckets and kneeling to pray. These were Jane Addams' neighbors. Some of these people had attended the city's first kindergarten at Hull House as children themselves. Now grown, they held their own children's hands. Some of them were the young men who had deserted rough gangs to join in the games and theatrics at Hull House. Some of them remembered how their parents had learned skills in the classes at Hull House. Others had learned to speak English. All of them remembered the good that Hull House and Jane Addams had done.

One young grandniece of Jane Addams had never been to Hull House before the funeral. She looked around her curiously and asked: "Are we all Aunt Jane's children?" In a sense, they were.

A country girl

Laura Jane Addams was the youngest child of John Huy and Sarah Weber Addams. She was born on

Opposite, top: John Huy Addams would always be a positive force in his youngest daughter's life. Many who knew John Addams admired him as an honest, generous man whose ideas were often ahead of their time.

Opposite, bottom: Using local labor and materials, John Addams built the big house in Cedarville, Illinois, where Jane Addams grew up. It still stands on a tree-lined street of the village and, although designated as a historic site, it has been used in recent years as a private home.

September 6, 1860, shortly before the Civil War began. By the time Jane was born, her ancestors had lived in America for more than two hundred years. In fact, the Addams family was one of those granted land by William Penn, the founder of the colony that would become the modern state of Pennsylvania.

The beliefs of this old and respected family strongly influenced Jane Addams' work. The Addams family, like many in this area, followed the Quaker faith. Quakers valued hard work. They believed in change through peaceful efforts. Above all, they had faith in the basic goodness of people. Although Jane did not practice the Quaker faith, she honored its teachings all her life.

John Addams, a miller by trade, married Sarah Weber in 1844. Excited by tales of boundless opportunity from relatives in Illinois, the young couple set out to "the frontier." They traveled by way of Chicago, which was then a town of eight thousand people. Built on soggy mud flats and named for the Indian word for "wild onion," Chicago did not suit John and Sarah Addams. Instead, they headed north into wide-open territory. There they found rich black soil ripe for wheat, hay, oats, and corn.

This, they decided, would make fine miller's land. So six miles (10 km) north of Freeport, Illinois, Sarah and John Addams bought a six-year-old gristmill set on eighty acres (32 ha) of woodland. There, in the village of Cedarville, they eventually built a two-story gray brick house where Jane Addams lived. The house — a tribute to her father's building skills — still stands and is still a family home.

Jane's parents did well. In upcoming years, John Addams would lead the movement to build a railroad through northern Illinois and become, as a bank owner, businessman, and state legislator, "the best-known man in the district."

A motherless little girl

Jane Addams had a happy childhood, but it was marked by personal loss. Before she was three years old, her mother, a lively and intelligent woman, died after giving birth to a stillborn baby. Jane's teenage sisters, Mary, Martha, and Alice, took over the "mothering" of the young girl, whom everyone called Jenny.

They told her tales of their mother, whose lessons had left marked imprints on her children. In one story, young Weber Addams, the only brother, was playing near the rushing water of the millrace. This was something all the Addams children had been forbidden to do. Appearing suddenly, Sarah Addams pushed her son into the water. As his sisters watched in terror, Weber struggled helplessly. At the last instant, his mother ran to a bend in the stream and pulled the sputtering boy out. After that, no one ever had to explain the dangers of the millrace again.

A strong bond

Without a mother's guidance, little Jane became something of a tomboy. She also became her father's pet. But Jane, in return, idolized her father. To her, he embodied everything good and wise. He had no faults. He was the source from which both her memories and her values sprang. In short, he was the force that shaped her entire life.

John Addams found respect even beyond his daughter's worshipful eyes. People knew him as an honest, intensely curious man who loved books and

As this photo of six-year-old Jane Addams suggests, she was a shy, introspective child. Already motherless at this age, Jane depended heavily on her father and her older sisters and brother. When her sister Martha died — about the time this photograph was taken — Jane grew even more attached to her father.

ideas. Many of these fine characteristics he passed along to his famous daughter.

He was also known to have an independent mind. As a sensible businessman, John Addams contributed to every church in town but joined none. He described himself as a "Hicksite Quaker," after Elias Hicks, a New York Quaker who became famous for preaching of the "inner light" as a guide for behavior. To John Addams, the "inner light" meant accepting other people's ways, personal integrity, and democracy. Because of these beliefs, then, it was no surprise that Addams hated slavery. He became a staunch abolitionist. When the Civil War broke out, Addams, as a Quaker, was forbidden to fight. But he did help raise and outfit a local regiment.

Daughter Jane took these lessons as her own moral compass. Years down the road, her views and actions would be just as controversial as they were praiseworthy. But people's opinions did not influence her choices. Calmly and assuredly, she simply listened to her inner voice and counted on her own good sense. Near the end of her life, Addams would one day help found the American Civil Liberties Union to underscore her belief in diversity of thought.

Never exactly carefree

Jane Addams was a dreamy child and something of a loner. She loved best of all to play in the dusky recesses of the mill, making her version of "mud pies" with the piles of bran. People who knew her described her as a pretty child. But Jane saw herself as "ugly" or, at the very least, "plain." This description no doubt grew out of her self-consciousness over a spinal problem that she suffered from. The condition, which was often painful, gave her a slightly curved spine and a pigeon-toed walk. All in all, Jane was a happy child who loved life. But perhaps because she had learned some hard lessons of life early, she was never exactly carefree.

One such lesson came when Jane was only four years old. On this dark day, Jane surprised her father in his bedroom. He was crying. Addams told his daughter that President Abraham Lincoln had been assassinated, saying that the "greatest man in the world" was dead. Lincoln, another midwesterner, was John

"He was a leader as well as a safe and fearless advocate of right things in public life. My own vivid recollection of John H. Addams is the fact that he was a man of purest and sternest integrity."
Jane Addams, of her father

"I found my father in tears, something I had never seen before, having assumed, as all children do, that grown-up people never cried."
Jane Addams

11

Right: Abraham Lincoln, shown here in one of the few portraits showing him beardless, was a longtime friend of John Addams. The two men met and became friends when both became involved in Illinois politics.

Below: Mourners in Chicago walk beside the funeral procession of Illinois' most famous son, Abraham Lincoln, in 1865. Although she was only four years old at the time, Jane Addams would never forget the day in April 1865 when Lincoln died.

Addams' idol and close friend. Over the years of their friendship, the two men had written to each other often. All her life, Jane Addams would treasure Lincoln's letters, which her father had kept in a little packet in his desk. Each began: "My dear Double-D'ed Addams." The sixteenth president respected Addams' opinion and sought it regularly.

Lincoln's death touched Jane Addams even more than had the death of her mother, whom she hardly remembered. Not long after came yet another crippling blow. Jane's sister Martha, sixteen years old and the prettiest of the Addams girls, died of typhoid fever. The family, and John Addams in particular, reeled from the shock of these losses.

Out into the world

When Jane was only six years old, she visited Freeport, Illinois, with her father. Jane was always pleased to spend time with her father, and she was looking forward to a visit to the candy store. This trip, however, was a trip she would remember always. Arriving in Freeport, Jane was puzzled when her father detoured down a side street. The scene awaiting the travelers alarmed six-year-old Jane. The street was filled with garbage and houses that looked ready to tumble down at the slightest breeze. Children wearing torn, dirty shirts played in the mud.

"Papa," Jane asked quietly, "why do these people live in such horrid houses?"

"They are poor," her father explained. "They have no money for nicer houses."

Before long, John Addams had finished his errand. He bought Jane candy, as she had hoped. But the taste of it was soured for her by the memory of the ugly slum dwellings she had seen. On the way home, she was absorbed in thought. After a long time, she told her father, "When I am a grown woman, I am going to buy a big house. Then the poor children can come and play in my yard whenever they want." Years later, it would appear that Jane Addams had foretold her own future.

In the meantime, little Jane Addams, her hair in braids, began school. She was especially clever at arithmetic and geography and was always willing to help other children who didn't find their subjects as easy as she did. Although she was a good student, her father still tutored her at home. He especially encouraged her to read history. Afterward, he would give her quizzes and reward her with a few pennies for her correct answers.

But bribery may not have been necessary in Jane's case. She already showed much self-discipline. From early on, she took to getting up before dawn to read books — history and classics among them. Her father had done the same when he was young, and Jane wanted more than anything to be like her father.

A new family

In 1868, John Addams married Anna Haldeman, a widow. Anna Haldeman was a good-looking, rich, and accomplished woman. She and John Addams were a good match.

For years, Jane had been the center of her father's world. Like any other child, she disliked giving up this position to her stepmother. But eventually, the two families would blend into one. And eventually, Jane and her stepmother would come to accept each other.

Anna Addams was high-strung, forceful, and perhaps a bit of a nag. But along with her many talents, she did bring with her a bonus — a son, George, who was just Jane's age. Her stepbrother became her boon companion. Together they went to school, played in the mill, and explored the caves and hills around their home. With George, the bookish Jane learned an even greater love of nature. Jane often thought of these carefree days in later life while working with the children of Chicago's slums. It made her sad to think that they had never run in sunny fields or breathed in pure air.

As an adult, Jane Addams fondly remembered many evenings when she, George, and her stepmother would gather around the family table to read Shakespeare aloud. Each of them took parts in the plays. These evenings led to Jane's special attachment, years later at Hull House, to reading clubs as one way to encourage friendships.

The new Mrs. Addams had an older son, too — handsome, eighteen-year-old Harry Haldeman. Eight years later, Harry and Alice Addams touched off an

Although excitable and strong-willed, Anna Haldeman Addams (center) was a caring stepmother to John Addams' children. Here she is seen with her younger son, George, and Jane in about 1876.

explosion in the family. At the time, Alice was fresh from school at Rockford Seminary. Harry had also been away, studying in Europe. Suddenly, the two fell terribly in love. Both parents dug in against the affair, but Alice's and Harry's wills were a match for them. Eventually, the two young people married.

Once Anna Addams had accepted this marriage, however, she seemed determined that Jane should grow up to marry George. She put forth her opinions in no uncertain terms. However, Jane Addams was "too busy" to marry.

Years later, long after both her stepmother and George were dead, Jane Addams would sometimes amuse herself by sitting in on psychic gatherings. At these gatherings, "psychics" sitting in a circle around a table would try to contact the spirit world. A spirit, they said, would make its presence known through a series of taps on the table. Invariably, the first raps would address Jane Addams.

"Oh, it's my stepmother, of course, it always is," she would say casually, "still reproaching me for not having married George."

The seeds of her work

After the North won the Civil War, it began to concentrate its huge resources on industry. This shifted jobs, and, consequently, people, away from the sunny fields and into the raw, ill-planned cities. Powerful businessmen, industrialists, and bankers made fortunes on cheap labor, but the common workers suffered. The poor were often trampled in the rush for riches. And the U.S. government did little if anything to help. The government under President Ulysses S. Grant was so corrupt that businessmen could all but openly buy favors from congressmen. Jane, about thirteen years old at the time, understood very little of the way of the world. But these changes and problems were the seeds of the work she would one day do.

Meanwhile, Jane had become a shy, soft-spoken teenager. After graduating from high school in 1877, she hoped to attend Smith College in Massachusetts. When the time came, her father instead sent her to Rockford Seminary, where her sisters had gone. The fact that John Addams was on the seminary's governing board may have had something to do with this decision. But more likely, Addams enjoyed having his youngest child close to him, particularly as all his older children were now married and living on their own.

At seventeen, Jane Addams was off to Rockford Seminary. By this time, she had blossomed into an attractive young woman. In her mirror, however, Addams still saw herself as plain and skinny, with a nose that had "no character whatever, and [contained] eight freckles horrible to relate."

A woman's place

In the late 1800s, many Americans believed that a woman's place was in the home. Women were expected to learn to write with a "fine hand," paint on china, play the piano, and read well enough to keep up with their husbands' interests. Education for women beyond this was not common. But John Addams was ahead of his time in his ideas about education. He believed that girls as well as boys should have the opportunity to get a higher education.

Education was, in general, becoming a stronger force in American life. Between 1860 and 1880, five hundred high schools were established in the United States. But not until three years after Jane received her diploma from Rockford would the educational system really begin to change. Then a young man from Johns Hopkins University, John Dewey, would introduce ideas for making education useful instead of merely enlightening. Dewey, who became a leading philosopher, strongly influenced Jane Addams' work.

To school at Rockford

Rockford Seminary, chartered in 1847, was one of the oldest institutions of female education in the Mississippi Valley. It was a tightly knit, strongly religious school, dedicated to turning out "useful" female missionaries. The seminary's principal, Anna P. Sill, staunchly supported its religious goals to a point that Jane Addams considered annoying. "She does everything for . . . the love of God alone," Addams wrote in her diary, "and I do not like that." She would become a girl who thought for herself, relying on the strong core of her father's teaching.

However, in her first days as a college student, Jane Addams was a timid figure. She stood only five feet three inches (160 cm) tall and weighed just ninety-five pounds (43 kg). But in spite of her early shyness, she quickly became a favorite of the other girls.

"School girls are not psychologists," Corinne Williams Douglas, a Rockford schoolmate, wrote of

Young women attend a college physics class in the late 1800s. Studying science, Jane Addams often said, would help women turn their natural intuitiveness to practical application. In many speeches and papers she wrote while at Rockford Female Seminary, she urged women to develop habits of mental discipline that science would give them.

Although sometimes overshadowed by her brilliant friend, Ellen Gates Starr was an important figure in her own right. Their friendship led Starr to her role as cofounder of Hull House. There, she took a special interest in exposing the settlement's visitors to art. Starr believed that working-class people thirsted for beauty no less than those of the privileged classes.

Jane Addams, "and we never speculated as to why we liked to go to her room so that it was always crowded. We just knew that there was always something 'doing' where [Jane] was, and that however mopey it might be elsewhere there was intellectual ozone in her vicinity." Night after night during the school year, girls would gather in Jane's room, endlessly discussing and sorting out their destinies. To be useful was their goal, yes — but how?

Exploring new ideas

While searching for an answer, Addams turned her energies to her studies and grew in stature at Rockford. She became the editor of the school's literary magazine. She also earned a reputation as the school's most effective speechmaker. This talent, which would last all her life, eventually led her to participate in a debate contest with the brilliant William Jennings Bryan. In English class, she wrote that the world judges "not on what might have been . . . not on the motive or the effort put forth, but on solely what is." Already, she was preparing for a life of action, but not as a missionary, although the school tried to persuade many of the girls to choose this vocation. Dryly, Addams wrote in her diary, "The desirability of Turkey as a field for missionary labor was enticingly put before me." She would have no part of it.

In her first year at Rockford, Addams made a friend who would mean more to her than anything else gained at Rockford. The friend, Ellen Gates Starr, came from Durand, Illinois. More than a decade later, Ellen Gates Starr and Jane Addams would found Hull House together. But even while in school together, the two were a powerful force. There they collaborated on the bold goal of making Rockford a college, rather than a seminary. This included convincing the administration to offer courses that would make the young women's diplomas equal to that of any young man's.

Clearly an early feminist, Jane Addams wrote about concerns over women's place in American life. This concern would later carry her into the struggle for women's suffrage. She also encouraged girls to take up science so they could benefit from its training in hard, precise, objective thought.

But her college years were not all triumph for Addams. Her time at college also marked a period of doubt and puzzlement, as it is for so many young people today. Religion, in particular, was a topic that troubled her. As she tried to determine what she believed, she often confided her doubts to Ellen Gates Starr. At one point, Addams told Starr of an experiment in which she had given up all prayer for three months. To Addams' shock, she wrote that she felt "no worse for it." Religion would be something over which she struggled for years.

But not all of Addams' experiments were as harmless. Intrigued by British writer Thomas De Quincey's book *Confessions of an English Opium Eater*, she and four classmates decided to try opium for themselves. The girls felt that trying the drug, which was then much easier to obtain than it is today, would help them understand De Quincey's writing. Instead of wonderful experiences of the imagination, they felt nothing at all, Addams confessed. But a young teacher discovered their experiment, became alarmed, and took away both the opium and the De Quincey books. She then sent the students to their rooms, demanding that they present themselves for worship after dinner no matter how woozy they felt. This would be Jane Addams' one and only experiment with drugs.

Good-bye to Rockford
While at Rockford Seminary, Jane Addams gained an understanding of the world and the individual's place in it. And reading the words of contemporary writers such as John Ruskin, Matthew Arnold, and Thomas Carlyle, she saw that she was not alone in her questions and doubts concerning that place. This was perhaps her greatest gain from her college years.

Thoughts on the individual's place in the world often were closely tied to those on women's place. Planning her speech as Rockford's valedictorian and most honored graduate, Addams urged classmate Nora Frothingham, another speaker, "Let's SAY something, Nora." Addams chose as her text the legend of Cassandra, the Trojan prophet whose fate it was to speak the truth without ever being believed. She compared that fate to the lot of contemporary women.

Thomas De Quincey's book about opium addiction caught the interest of Jane Addams and four of her friends. To understand De Quincey's experiences, the young women experimented with the drug. It was Addams' one and only experiment with dangerous drugs.

Women, she said, must learn to focus their intuitive minds "so that [they] can face social ills and social problems as tenderly and as intuitively as [they] can now care for and understand a crippled factory child."

Shattered plans

Addams graduated from Rockford Seminary in June 1881. In the fall, she planned to go east and study medicine at the Women's Medical College of Philadelphia. But the darkest hours she was to know still lay between her and her shining goal.

On July 2, 1881, history rushed up to touch Jane Addams' life, as it would so often do in the future. That day, President James A. Garfield was shot in a Washington railroad station. For eleven weeks, the president struggled between life and death, but died on September 19. The assassin, Charles Guiteau, was the son of one of John Addams' bank employees. Guiteau's sister, Flora, was a family friend, and Jane stood by her all through her brother's trial and eventual execution. Not everyone approved of such loyalty, but that did not concern Jane Addams.

That August, John Addams had taken his family on a trip to Wisconsin and Michigan. Addams felt that the trip might ease the strain of the recent troubling events. Along the way, John Addams suddenly suffered a crippling attack of stomach pain. The family decided to return home at once but traveled only as far as a hotel in Green Bay, Wisconsin. There, at the age of fifty-nine, John Addams died of a ruptured appendix. In heartbroken silence, the family returned to Cedarville. There, John Huy Addams was buried.

Jane Addams was devastated by her father's death. She then realized how much she had depended on her father's love and support. Much of her courage and confidence came from that support. Without him, she felt hollow. But she knew that life must go on.

She also knew that her share of her father's estate — which was worth $350,000 — made her a wealthy woman. She would never have to worry about money again. So, since her stepbrother George was set to study medicine at Johns Hopkins, Addams decided to carry through with her plan to study at the Women's Medical College of Philadelphia.

Another setback

She entered the school in October 1881. But all too soon, she began to feel that medical school was not for her. And no sooner, it seemed, had Addams begun her course of study than her fragile health began to fail. For years she had endured back pain. But now, as she struggled to pass her exams in the spring, an even greater pain cut into her back. Her brother-in-law, Harry Haldeman, had become a physician. He called in a specialist to look at Jane. The specialist told Haldeman, "She'll not live a year."

"You don't know her," Dr. Haldeman replied. "She'll outlive us all."

Addams mustered the strength to return to Rockford and stand proudly to receive the degree she had earned a year before. By this time, Rockford Seminary had become Rockford College. The school could now award its students a college degree rather than just a certificate of completion.

Once at home, however, she collapsed. The pain of her father's death and what the doctors now diagnosed as an abscess on her spine crashed in on her. For her back, surgery was the only answer. Haldeman performed the surgery, which, although painful, was necessary. For six months afterward, she was confined to bed at the Haldeman home in Iowa, where she had to lie flat on her back.

After that, she was fitted with a heavy corset of leather, whalebone, and steel that extended from her neck to her hips. Addams wore the corset, which was meant to help support her healing back, for a year. The pain, frustration, and weariness of this whole period must have been great for Addams, who was at that time only twenty-two.

A tour of Europe

As Jane was recovering, her ever-energetic stepmother suggested that they take a tour of Europe. So when the ocean liner *Servia* set sail for Europe on August 22, 1883, Jane and Anna Addams were among its passengers. Although Jane was still in great pain, she refused to be held back by her illness. "Failure through ill health is just as . . . miserable as failure through any other cause," she wrote.

> *"It was quite settled in my mind that I should study medicine and 'live with the poor.'"*
>
> Jane Addams

On her first European tour, Jane Addams saw terrible poverty: people wearing ragged clothing, sleeping in public parks, and fighting like animals over rotten food. Memories of this trip would later inspire her to visit Toynbee Hall, an Oxford-based settlement that served as a model for Hull House.

In the late 1800s, many wealthy Americans took similar tours of Europe. Young women, in particular, often journeyed to Europe after college and before marriage. Americans still felt their pioneer roots were a disadvantage while Europe was the center of culture. But Jane Addams had hardly set foot on European soil when she was struck by the painful social realities of the bustling industrial countries there. Late one Saturday night in London, the travelers — Addams, her stepmother, and several other friends — went into the slums near Mile End Road. Wretched, haggard women and children fought in a mob at an open-air market. Everyone was scrambling frantically to buy rotten vegetables that middle-class families would have thrown away in disgust. Addams was haunted for the rest of her life by the memory of the outstretched hands that night on Mile End Road.

Throughout her trip, Addams was appalled by well-to-do Europeans' attitude toward the suffering and poor people in their midst. In Coburg, Germany, she curtly asked a brewery owner if something could be done to help his workers. From her hotel, she had seen female brewery workers struggling beneath tanks of scalding-hot beer. When she spoke to the owner, he reacted with "exasperating indifference." It puzzled him that anyone should care about these women's pain. It was part of their jobs, he told Addams. To him, they were of no more concern than cart horses.

Jane and Anna Addams toured Europe for nearly two years. Jane dutifully recorded the shopping, the

"We may not be able to 'change human nature' but we do hope to modify human behavior."

Jane Addams

museum visits, the fashionable suppers, and the theater dates. But an idea was growing in her head all the while. What good was fine art and culture if it did not inspire people to greater humanity? What good was all her education if it did not inspire her to service?

A long search

At home again in 1885, Addams suffered what might have been called, in her time, "nervous exhaustion." Today, it would probably be diagnosed as depression. While recovering, she found herself searching for her life's purpose.

She had always been a busy, involved person. Even now, in a very confusing period of her life, she remained so. She continued to study and read, she attended lectures and theater events, and she participated in certain clubs and charitable organizations. But nothing lifted her spirits.

In 1887, Addams turned twenty-seven years old. She felt she had done little to fulfill the goals she had envisioned for herself at Rockford. All her attempts at independence were failures, she wrote to Starr, who was now a schoolteacher. She went on to say: "I wish I had a call to foreign missions as some of the girls at Rockford had. They knew what they wanted to do."

A purpose at last

Restlessly, Addams traveled to Europe again in late 1887. This time, she joined Ellen Gates Starr, who had gone there on vacation from her art classes in Chicago. In Madrid, what started out as an evening of simple distraction became an event of great significance for Addams. That evening, the young women attended a bullfight. The sensitive Starr was quickly horrified by the sport and left. Afterward, Addams was shocked to realize that she had actually enjoyed the spectacle. She searched her conscience. Had all her seeking of culture only dulled her sympathies? Addams determined that night to use her life to make a difference in the world.

One month later, she visited Toynbee Hall in the brutally poor Whitechapel district of London's East End. There, a group of Oxford scholars had "moved in" to try to counteract some of the pitiful effects of the country's industrialization. The settlement was an

While still casting about for her life's purpose, Jane Addams toured Europe for a second time. In Germany, this cathedral in the city of Ulm awed her. There, she later wrote, she had a vision of a "cathedral of humanity," where people of many backgrounds would work together toward freedom and peace.

23

experiment in translating Christian values into social action. There, a variety of people lived among the poor residents. Their goal was to better understand the needs of the poor people and help them improve their conditions however they could. The benefit was mutual. Shared experience and understanding would improve urban life for everyone.

Already, the Toynbee experiment was making its way to America in the form of New York's Neighborhood Guild. Soon it would find its most vivid expression at Hull House. Hull House would be a settlement house like Toynbee Hall, but it would be located in Addams' own native Illinois, in the sprawling city of Chicago.

The plan unfolds

When they returned from Europe, Jane Addams explained her plan to Ellen Gates Starr. Starr embraced the plan with characteristic confidence. Together, the young women returned to the city that journalist Lincoln Steffens described as "first in violence, deepest in dirt, loud, lawless, unlovely, ill-smelling. Criminally, it was wide-open; socially it was thoughtless and raw." It was Chicago.

By the late 1800s, the city population had reached one million. And each day, more immigrants poured in, many of them fleeing the poverty of their homelands. Among those there were nearly half a million German

Most of Hull House's neighbors lived in wooden shacks such as these. These horrid dwellings were firetraps that lacked proper plumbing and provided little shelter from either the winter cold or the summer heat. These conditions made the slums perfect breeding grounds for disease.

people, a quarter of a million people from Ireland, and thousands of Swedes, Italians, Polish Jews, Russians, Scandinavians, and Greeks. All of these people clustered in a city that did not know how to provide anything for them except the chance to work for slave wages. Still, Chicago welcomed these people — with a sneer.

Struggling in a new land

Very few immigrants found much to improve their situations. All too often life in the crowded city worsened things. For although they had been poor in their native countries, they had remained proud. But the terrible conditions in cities like Chicago often took even that from them. Here greedy industrialists preyed upon the vulnerable mass of immigrants as a ready source of cheap labor.

Conditions in their factories were bad enough. But the poor wages the factory owners paid these people forced many of them to live in equally bad situations. Many lived in rickety, rat-infested tenement houses. There, their ever-growing numbers resulted in overcrowding. These conditions, coupled with the rotting garbage and filth that clogged the streets and

In the late 1800s, thousands of immigrants poured into the country each day. To deal with this mass of people, the government established an immigration center on Ellis Island in New York Harbor in 1892. The center closed in 1954, having processed over twenty million immigrants in sixty-two years of operation. It has since been restored and reopened as an immigration museum.

alleys, made a perfect breeding ground for diseases such as cholera and tuberculosis.

On top of this, many Americans — whose own ancestors had come from other lands — didn't trust "foreigners." They considered them sneaky, crude, and morally low. Even the immigrants didn't trust each other. To make matters worse, there was widespread distrust between workers and employers. The needs of the common laborer were not given much consideration. For example, when workers at the McCormick Reaper Company requested an eight-hour workday in 1886, they were denied. A strike followed. During a labor demonstration in Haymarket Square on May 4, police opened fire on the crowd. A bomb was then thrown into police lines and a bloody riot, known as the Haymarket Riot, followed. Seven people died.

Finding a house

Into this angry city, worn by poverty and torn by violence, came the two young women. But here was as fertile a field for Jane Addams' plan as earth could have provided. She and Starr only needed to find a place to begin their work. With their sense of mission sharp, Addams and Starr went in search of a house.

They found it on the corner of Halsted and Polk streets. There stood a two-story red brick mansion that had once been the country home of Charles J. Hull. Hull built the house in 1856, before the city began to sprawl west from its center near Lake Michigan. By 1889, when Addams and Starr found it, the mansion had lost some of its original beauty as the neighborhood had declined. It now stood between a saloon on one side and a funeral parlor on the other.

When Addams and Starr entered Hull House, they saw past the sagging woodwork encrusted with grimy paint. They had found it! This was the house for which they had searched. Although they could rent only those rooms not being used for other purposes, the two women were satisfied. Eventually, Helen Culver, Charles Hull's heir and the owner of Hull House, would allow Addams the use of the whole house. Later she stopped charging the settlement rent. In the end, she gave Addams the entire house, along with some surrounding land.

Opposite: Immigrant families, such as this one arriving at New York City's Ellis Island, came by the thousands to Chicago. There they were swept up in the cruelties of newly industrialized America, where factory owners learned that each wave of desperate immigrants would work for even cheaper wages.

"In 1892 the condition of the alleys was such that epidemic cholera seemed inevitable. During that summer residents at Hull House forwarded to the Board of Health more than one thousand complaints of violations of the sanitary laws."
Florence Kelley,
Hull House supporter

"Hull-House itself is a spacious mansion, with all its rooms opening, American fashion, into each other. There are no doors, or, more exactly, no shut doors; the residents wander from room to room, visitors wander here, there and everywhere."
Beatrice Webb,
English social reformer

The tense political climate that existed in Chicago after the Haymarket Riot — in which striking workers clashed with police — affected life at Hull House. Jane Addams would turn no one away from Hull House dinners or discussion groups. She believed everyone had a right to speak.

After several months of work on the house, Addams, Starr, and housekeeper Mary Keyser moved into it on the evening of September 18, 1889. It was the fulfillment of a dream that Addams later described this way: "I gradually became convinced that it would be a good thing to rent a house in a part of the city where many primitive . . . needs are found, in which young women who have been given over too exclusively to study might . . . learn of life itself."

That night, as the six-year-old Jane had promised, she became the woman living in the big house among all the "horrid" little houses, as she had called them. And now — finally — she would be able to invite the poor children to play in her yard.

Working against the skeptics

Not everyone was immediately impressed with Addams' plans — especially some of her relatives. Yes, they agreed, the desire to help was all well and good. But to actually live in the slums was unheard of for an unmarried young woman from a good family. Anna Addams was not at all pleased with Jane's plan and flatly refused to contribute a penny to it. Others, while impressed by Hull House's goals, were skeptical that it could succeed. Addams asked one such doubter, sharply, "You think I'm trying to scoop out the ocean with a teaspoon, don't you?"

Even the area's residents — the people for whom Addams had created the settlement — were suspicious at first. Why were two wealthy and educated young women living in the old Hull house? Local priests warned their flocks that the two new neighbors were probably heathens intent on converting them to a new religion. Tough young street children threw garbage on the newly swept steps and pitched rocks through the windows.

But the founders of Hull House did not give up easily. Addams and Starr continued to greet the neighbors in a friendly way. At first, people came out of curiosity. But soon, they discovered that the young women of Hull House were very nice. The neighborhood women began to visit more freely.

Hunger was another factor that originally brought many visitors to the house. Hungry children learned that milk and spaghetti could be purchased for a penny at the house. On winter nights, weary adult workers found that the Hull House kitchen provided nourishing bowls of soup for a nickel or a dime. And all year round, the settlement offered companionship to all who passed through its doors. The neighborhood people quickly realized that Hull House could help

"[Hull House's] faith was humanism. It 'warmed both hands before the fire of life.' No newcomer could resist its ease, its tolerance, or its cordiality."

Francis Hackett, Hull House resident

Although the immigration center on Ellis Island closed in 1954, people continue to immigrate to the United States even today. Here, arriving Soviet Jews are greeted by relatives at Kennedy International Airport in New York City.

A rare photo shows young Jane Addams (right) with Hull House cofounder Ellen Gates Starr (left) and one of the settlement's many young volunteers. In the early days, Addams paid for all of Hull House's needs out of her own pocket. Later, benefactors helped fund the budget that, by the 1920s, had reached nearly $100,000 a year.

"We have always held strongly to the doctrine of nonresistance, selecting the good in the neighborhood and refraining from railing at the bad."

Jane Addams

---

them make sense of their terrible lot. The people began to depend on the settlement. Soon, it would become the center of their daily activities.

Hull House finds its niche

In its first years, Hull House established the city's first day-care center. Jane Addams had heard agonizing tales of working mothers. Many women, in order to work, were forced to leave their babies unattended, often for ten hours or more. One story told of a mother who, desperate to keep her tiny child from harm, had tied the child to a table leg with a bowl of porridge within reach. Addams knew these mothers' heartache. But she also knew that leaving children alone was a dangerous thing. She convinced a wealthy woman to finance a day-care center in a cottage near Hull House. Working mothers paid five cents a day to have their children cared for at the center. But if they could not afford the fee, they paid nothing.

But Addams did more than help people with their needs. She went on to help them improve their self-esteem. Instead of criticizing the immigrants' foreign ways, Jane Addams welcomed them. Her goal was to "preserve and keep for them whatever of value their past life contained and to bring them in contact with a better type of American." Many immigrant groups were surprised to find the other Hull House residents eager to help them celebrate their culture. The holidays of the individual nations caused great excitement, and rooms were decorated in national colors. Weddings and funerals were held there, too.

People at Hull House seemed as eager to learn about other cultures as they were to share their own. The Germans came on Friday nights to sing songs of their homeland or recite poetry written by the German Johann Wolfgang von Goethe. Other nights were reserved for interests of Italian and Irish people. At Ellen Starr's urging, the people drank in poetry, literature, and art. The ideas that Addams and Starr had gained while in Europe were finally being put to use.

It works!

Trying to help less fortunate people with spaghetti and poetry seemed such a foolish idea. Perhaps because it was so simple, it worked. In a public address on the topic, Jane said, "It is constantly said that because the masses have never had social advantages they do not

Jane Addams believed in taking pride in one's cultural heritage. Her thoughts are echoed by the cultural festivities (above and below) that continue throughout the United States today.

ACT WELL YOUR PART. THERE ALL THE HONOUR LIES.

Hull House was credited with helping to start Chicago's "little theater" movement. Some of the settlement's performances drew nationwide notice. After seeing a Hull House production of his play Justice, *British writer John Galsworthy allowed the settlement to stage a world premiere of another of his plays.*

"It has been the aim of the residents to respond to all sides of the neighborhood life; not to the poor people alone, nor to the well-to-do, nor to the young in contradistinction to the old, but to the neighborhood as a whole."
Jane Addams

want them, that they are heavy and dull, and it will take political . . . machinery to change them." For some of the families, however, it took far less.

In just a few years' time, Hull House was involved in countless projects. A kindergarten was opened in the playroom. In 1891, the Jane Club began. This cooperative boarding home for working women was the first of its kind in the United States. When a wealthy patron offered Jane several buildings in the neighborhood, she gratefully accepted, and then asked permission to tear them down. The nation's first public playground was born.

In the evenings, young immigrant men and women came for college extension courses. Workmen relaxed in the social science club, discussing the evils of government and rich employers or debating with a civic leader who had come to speak to them that night. Addams believed that these spirited nights actually quelled labor unrest by allowing people to speak their minds. Socialists, radicals, Republicans, and Democrats were all welcome. The host asked only that the different groups hear one another out.

A need for volunteers

The success of the venture brought huge demands for help. Eventually, more than one hundred full- or part-time workers gave their time to the settlement. At least twenty of these people actually lived at Hull House. Among them were many of the overprivileged young women Addams and Starr had first hoped to attract. Many of these educated young people had been "shut off from the common labor by which they live," Jane Addams said in a famous lecture in Plymouth, Massachusetts, just three years after Hull House opened.

Soon, these women were up to their elbows in "real life" experiences. They bathed babies, cared for the sick, taught classes, and acted as translators. Just as Addams and Starr did, these volunteers did whatever they could to help the immigrants sort out the mysteries of life in this new land.

Among those devoted to Hull House were Julia Lathrop, Florence Kelley, Louise De Koven Bowen,

"Hull-House teemed with ideas. . . . The adult English classes for foreigners were based upon leftover Sears Roebuck catalogues. . . . The little theatre was rampant with talent. The music school was an eyrie of singing birds."
Victor Weybright,
editor and author

Unlike many native-born Americans, Jane Addams did not scorn the arts and traditions of her foreign-born neighbors. Instead, she embraced them. At Hull House, Addams encouraged demonstrations of lost arts such as spinning, hoping to increase the immigrants' pride in their origins.

Mary Rozet Smith, one of Hull House's tireless supporters, became one of Jane Addams' closest friends. The women were so close that Smith's death in 1934 plunged Addams into one of the worst depressions of her life.

"Jane's idea, which she puts very much to the front, . . . is that it [settlement work] is more for the benefit of the people who do it than for the other class. Jane feels that . . . one gets as much as she gives."

Ellen Gates Starr, cofounder
of Hull House

Alice Hamilton, and Mary Rozet Smith. This group of women — along with Starr and Addams — helped Hull House become the powerful institution it became. Many of these women also brought about changes outside of their work at Hull House. But perhaps best of all, this group helped to awaken the social conscience of the country.

Alice Hamilton, a doctor, eventually went on to work in industrial medicine, uncovering dangerous practices that risked workers' lives. Her studies brought about changes that improved factory conditions. She also supervised a study of Chicago's fly-ridden slums and their role in a typhoid epidemic.

Julia Lathrop made public welfare her specialty. Louise De Koven Bowen used her wealth to build Bowen Hall, the meeting place for the Woman's Club. She later used her influence to help establish the nation's first juvenile court — a system that recognized that young people who went wrong needed help rather than punishment. Mary Rozet Smith became one of Jane Addams' closest lifelong friends. Smith opened her lavish home to settlement residents.

Fighting the sweatshops

Florence Kelley made sweatshop operations her focus. Sweatshops were one of the greatest shames of the industrial age. In this system, manufacturers had workers producing goods out of their homes or other locations rather than out of the factories. Sometimes the shop was no more than a dank stable or a dark basement. There, sweatshop workers — primarily women and children — worked long hours and were paid only for the number of completed items. Often little girls as young as seven or eight years old sewed fancy dress trousers for seven cents a dozen. Sweatshops produced all types of goods, but clothing provided the bulk of the work. This system increased production while keeping manufacturers' costs low because extra factory space was not needed.

Kelley went to work for the Illinois State Bureau of Labor investigating the sweatshops. She marched on the sweatshops, exposing the ugly truth. Her work helped improve the sweatshop operations and brought about child labor laws. Under the first factory law in Illinois, women and girls were restricted to eight-hour workdays. The law also stated that children under the age of fourteen were not to work in factories and needed a special permit to work at all.

Hull House established a housing project for single working women that was the first of its kind in the United States. Known as the Jane Club, this project provided large, decent apartments for cooperative living.

A new job

Six years after opening Hull House, Jane Addams became, of all things, the garbage inspector for Chicago's Nineteenth Ward. Her appointment came about after local residents began complaining about the garbage situation in the ward. For although the city had hired garbage collectors, the dirt-packed streets rolled in filth. Garbage boxes along the streets overflowed. On top of this, merchants and private households dumped their wastes everywhere and anywhere. Without regular collection, the mounds of rotting debris bred rats and disease.

When complaints and reports did no good, Addams herself applied for the job of ward garbage collector. Although she did not win this position, city officials named her the ward's garbage inspector. For Addams, this added responsibility meant rising each morning at dawn. Her job included walking behind the garbage wagons to force the angry trash collectors to take care of the garbage properly.

Sickness and recovery

Before she had been at this new position for a year, Addams was hit hard with typhoid fever. Perhaps her work in the streets had something to do with it, but, more likely, the six years of endless work was to blame. In time, she began to recover, but the illness left her weak, and her progress was slow. Her doctor demanded that she rest. With the hectic pace of life at Hull House, Addams knew she would recover faster if she could get away for a while. When a Hull House assistant secured the position of ward garbage inspector, Addams felt free to leave.

In 1896, Addams sailed once more for Europe. This time, Mary Rozet Smith accompanied her. One of the highlights of the trip was a visit to Moscow, where the women arranged to meet Leo Tolstoy. Tolstoy, the Russian author of influential novels such as *War and Peace*, had been born a wealthy count. He was also known as a humanitarian. His concern for the world's poor people had caused him to renounce all his wealth and live as a peasant.

To Addams' surprise, Tolstoy criticized her. The fashionable sleeves of her dress, he told her, contained enough material to make a dress for a little girl. Addams took Tolstoy's words seriously. But she also tried to explain that her sleeves were small compared with those of the working women in Chicago. She also pointed out that nothing would separate her more from the people than wearing clothing that was different from their own. Tolstoy was not convinced.

Back to work

Back at Hull House, Jane Addams tried to follow Tolstoy's example and do more chores around Hull House — particularly bread baking. As a miller's daughter, she had done this task with ease since the age of twelve. But these new tasks only added to the demands on Addams. She quickly realized that her time would be better used fighting larger battles. And a great many of those lay just ahead in the dawn of the new century.

Leo Tolstoy was a Russian writer and philosopher. Although born into the upper class, Tolstoy came to believe in equality for all people. In 1876, he gave up his wealth to live as a peasant, putting his beliefs into practice. As a writer, Tolstoy is perhaps best remembered for War and Peace, *and he is considered one of the world's literary giants.*

Historian Allen F. Davis writes that people who remember Addams "as a kindly social worker and gentle pacifist should [recall] Jane Addams the realistic reformer who battled Johnny Powers in the Nineteenth Ward." John Powers was Chicago's enormously influential Nineteenth Ward alderman. Rich and swaggering, Powers was just like so many other factory and slum owners who handed out petty favors to the immigrants while somehow controlling their shamefully poor lives. In Powers' case, for example, he sometimes treated workingmen to a beer, but it was he who owned the saloons where they later squandered their paychecks. For one immigrant, he paid a hospital bill. He gave another a Christmas turkey, a handful of cigars, or a lavish wedding gift. But these favors were not given unconditionally. In return, Powers expected the loyalty — and the vote — of the neighborhood people.

Into this comfortable setting came Jane Addams. She challenged the "right" of "the boss" to buy people's goodwill so cheaply while stuffing his pockets with rents and bribes.

"Why does Jane Addams attack me?" Powers asked anyone who would listen. "Aren't we both working to help the immigrants?"

By 1910, when this photograph was taken, the Hull House settlement had outgrown the original mansion. Eventually the settlement would include thirteen buildings. Two of these original buildings still stand and make up the Jane Addams Hull House Museum.

Hull House Settlement, Chicago.

Addams replied that Powers was making a fortune out of the slums while she was not. She continued to challenge his rule and, together with other Hull House members, sought to remove him from office. Powers sneered at Addams' attempts, threatening, "Hull House will be driven from the ward!" In the end, Powers won reelection and stayed in the ward. But so did Hull House — and its influence grew.

Poor conditions continue

At the beginning of the twentieth century, Chicago's common people still faced immense problems. A work week averaged fifty-nine hours; pay was about ten dollars a week for a man. Back then, as now, women made even less. Many earned barely a dollar for a twelve-hour day. To get by, many families still needed their children to work. Living and working conditions remained horrible.

By this time, because of her work, Addams was seen as the protector of the common people. She believed in their rights and spoke her mind on their behalf. She allowed labor unions to meet at Hull House. Because of her beliefs, Addams developed a wide circle of influential friends. This group included journalists like Lincoln Steffens, who dug up stories of the corruption on the floor of American life and presented it in vivid detail to horrified readers.

Socialist Eugene V. Debs was another of Jane Addams' friends. At this time, the socialist movement had gained ground in the country. Socialists believed, in part, in equality, social justice, and a system of public ownership. The socialist movement in the United States demanded better living conditions for poor people, honesty in government, and less power for the wealthy. But many Americans considered socialism a dangerous system.

Addams' own style was less dramatic than that of many of her friends. When delivering a speech, she always folded her hands, speaking logically and unemotionally. But with her quiet style, she often spoke the hardest truths. And, as always, she backed her words with action. For instance, although she understood the immigrants' need to send their young children out to work, she deplored this practice and

"Our effort at Hull-House has always been to seize upon the highest moral efforts we could find in the labor movement or elsewhere, and help them forward — to conserve the best which the community has achieved and push it forward along its own line when possible."
Jane Addams

Opposite: The faces of these tiny workers reflect the tragedy of the working world in the early twentieth century. Before child labor laws, children as young as these fish-market workers in Port Royal, South Carolina, regularly worked ten-hour days.

39

spoke against it. She campaigned for child labor laws and laws that made school attendance mandatory.

She also fought street gangs through Hull House's facilities and clubs. For this reason, a gymnasium was established at the settlement. She also urged the area children to join the Young Citizens' Club. Through this club, they were taught to use their frustration positively by reporting on conditions in the streets and alleys instead of making war on one another. The professional music classes at Hull House were yet another attraction for many youngsters. One of its participants grew up to be the famous clarinetist Benny Goodman. Addams believed these classes were more than just the pouring on of "culture." They were therapy for children beaten down by the conditions under which they lived. "It is good," she said, "for a social worker to be an artist, too."

Other projects

Addams did not limit her work to the Hull House neighborhood or even to the city of Chicago. Her mission of charity extended beyond Hull House. It led her to defend as well as befriend even the most controversial people. After President William McKinley was assassinated in 1901, many people expected Addams to keep anarchists — people who believe that government is unnecessary — away from Hull House. She didn't. In fact, she worked to free anarchist Abraham Issak, who had been unfairly imprisoned for his politics after the assassination. Issak, according to Addams, was a decent man.

That position cost her the friendship of one of her wealthiest admirers, Mrs. Potter Palmer, whose husband owned the glittering Palmer House hotel. But this was certainly not the first or last time that her work would bring trouble for Jane Addams. Later, she and her followers tried to organize women in the sewing trades into unions. Addams felt that these unions were necessary to secure better wages for the women. But this view made Addams unpopular in some powerful circles. So did her commitment to gaining for women the right to vote.

But no matter what people thought, Jane Addams held to her beliefs. No doubt she took comfort in her own words: "If we lose one group of friends by certain actions, we shall gain others."

Pushing for the vote

As the scope of Addams' activities widened, there seemed no end to the projects she undertook. Women's rights — particularly the right to vote — was one topic that she gave greater attention to again in the early twentieth century.

Addams enjoyed telling a story from her days as president of the National Conference of Social Work to show the need for equality for both blacks and women. As president of the group, she had persuaded President Theodore Roosevelt to call a White House conference on children. At the conference, an official called all the speakers to the platform.

"Are we all here?" he asked. "Yes, here is my Catholic speaker, my Jewish speaker, the Protestant, the colored man, and the woman." The "woman" in this case was Jane Addams; the "colored man" was educator Booker T. Washington.

"You see, I am last," Addams said to Washington. "That is because I have no vote."

A boatful of suffragists campaigns in New York Harbor in 1914. By this time, women had already won the battle for the vote, at least for local officials in Chicago and various other cities and states. But it would be another six years before the Nineteenth Amendment extended full voting rights to all adult citizens.

Booker T. Washington appeared with Jane Addams on many speakers' platforms. Washington, who was born a slave, grew up to write his pioneering autobiography Up From Slavery. *As an educator, he was a force in starting black colleges and was a leading black speaker in his time.*

To that, Washington replied, "I am glad to know the reason. I have always been at the end of such a procession myself."

Addams believed deeply in suffrage, or the right to vote. She insisted that denying the dignity of some demeaned the dignity of all. In 1907, in spite of her busy life at Hull House, she chaired the Committee for Municipal Suffrage for Women and led trainloads of delegates to Springfield to speak to the governor. Six years later, the group met with some success. That year, the city of Chicago extended local voting rights to all, regardless of sex. But full voting privileges for all levels of government were not secured for all American women until August 26, 1920, through the approval of the Nineteenth Amendment.

Farther into politics

Although she hardly ever took sides in politics, Addams joined the Progressive party in 1912. This newly formed party was backing Theodore Roosevelt for a third term in office. Addams joined the party when Roosevelt announced his support for both labor reform and women's right to vote.

"When a great party pledges itself to the protection of children, to the care of the aged, to the relief of overworked girls, to the safeguarding of burdened men, it is inevitable that it should appeal to women," Addams wrote to friends who said politics was no place for a woman. She was invited, in fact, to second Roosevelt's nomination at the Progressive convention, held in Chicago in August 1912. But when she heard that the Progressive party was attempting to exclude African-American delegates, she spoke out strongly against the practice.

It was rumored that, if elected, Roosevelt would offer Jane Addams a cabinet post. To this Roosevelt quickly replied, "I think she is so much more needed . . . at Hull House." In the end, Roosevelt lost the election to the Democratic candidate, Woodrow Wilson. Although Addams was disappointed, she felt that the time she spent campaigning had been time well spent. It had given her the opportunity to bring reform issues to an even greater audience.

The world at war

It was surprising, given all she did, that Jane Addams found time to write. In 1910, her moving book *Twenty Years at Hull House* became a best-seller. It seemed that Jane Addams had made her mark in life. But she was about to enter a phase of her career that would make her name known not only throughout Chicago but also around the world.

For some time before this, the European continent had become gradually divided into two extremely proud and jealous armed camps. The system of alliances among these countries was like a pile of dried sticks waiting for a fateful spark. On June 28, 1914, the spark was struck with the assassination of Austrian archduke Franz Ferdinand by a Serbian. In a matter of weeks, virtually all of Europe was at war. One side, the Central Powers, included Germany, Austria-Hungary, and Turkey. The other, known as the Allies, included Britain, France, and Russia.

Jane Addams was horrified. Her Quaker upbringing

"Look up, not down—
Look out, not in—
Look forward, not backward—
And lend a hand."

Founders' Day
October 27, 1912
THE
Progressive Party

A 1912 Progressive party campaign poster. Theodore Roosevelt organized this new party, which was also known as the Bull Moose party, and became its presidential candidate. The Progressive party appealed to many people like Jane Addams because of its interest in social reform.

Jane Addams was among the leaders of a delegation that traveled to The Hague during World War I for a peace conference. The mission marked the beginning of Addams' international role in peace work. Despite such efforts, the United States was drawn into the horrible conflict in 1917.

cried out for the nations to find peace through reason and compromise. As early as 1904, she had begun speaking out on pacifism. This belief opposes war or violence as means of settling disagreements.

"It is easy to kill a man," Addams told representatives of national peace societies at a convention in Boston. "It is not easy to bring him forward in the paths of civilization." As the war in Europe raged, the tales of trench warfare and the horrors of poison gas threw Addams into torment. To voice her concern, she journeyed to Washington in January 1915. There, she joined a group of about three thousand women who had gathered to organize the Woman's Peace party. The group, which elected Addams its chairperson, marched through the city carrying a banner that read "Real Patriots Keep Cool."

A fall from grace

That same year, Addams gave a speech that damaged her reputation. In April, she and forty other Americans had set sail aboard the SS *Noordam*, bound for a peace congress in the Netherlands, at The Hague. She returned on July 5 and was greeted warmly in New York City. A few days later, she gave a speech at Carnegie Hall.

She told her audience of the horrors of war. Some of the things she spoke of had been told directly to her by soldiers coming from the front. One such fact, Addams said, was that many of the young soldiers needed to be drugged with rum or ether to "perform the bloody work of bayonet charges."

Although Addams had used this fact to illustrate how senseless war is, people saw it as an insult to the soldiers. The speech brought Addams immediate and sharp criticism from all quarters. That the fact was true seemed of no importance. Richard Harding Davis, a popular novelist who considered himself an authority on warfare, was a leader in the attack on Addams. He wrote, "This insult, flung by a complacent and self-satisfied woman at men who gave their lives . . . I protest." Davis' rebuttal launched a newspaper war against Addams in which she was accused of demeaning brave young men.

Although she staunchly backed her words, Addams' immense popularity faltered. The disapproval grew so bad that after a speech at a church in Chicago, the audience refused to applaud her. A crushing blow came that day from Orrin Carter, chief justice of the Illinois Supreme Court. When the audience remained silent, Carter, a longtime friend and supporter of Addams, stood up.

"I have always been a friend of Miss Addams," Carter began, "but . . . "

"The 'but' sounds as if you were going to break with me," Addams said sharply.

Carter answered, "I am going to break with you."

On all sides, Jane Addams was blacklisted for her pacifist views. The Daughters of the American Revolution (DAR) had once honored Jane Addams, a DAR member, because of her colonial ancestry. The group now expelled her. Addams remarked dryly that she had understood that her membership was good for life. Now she was told that it was only during "good behavior." Even Addams' old friend Theodore Roosevelt called the Woman's Peace party "silly and base." He added angrily, "Pacifists are cowards."

But not everyone abandoned Addams during this terrible time. John Dewey, the famous American philosopher who had worked at Hull House during his

"[Jane Addams] utters instinctively the truth we others vainly seek."
William James, American philosopher and psychologist

Richard Harding Davis, a patriotic novelist and war reporter, led an attack on Jane Addams. In a speech, Addams revealed that many young soldiers were given liquor or other drugs to help them endure bayonet fighting. Davis called Addams' words an insult to brave young men.

University of Chicago days, supported the war. Yet he defended Addams, saying that her form of pacifism was not merely intended to help America mind its own business and stay out of trouble, as many people thought. Rather, he said, it presented a plan for positive interaction among nations that would improve conditions for all people.

The United States enters the war

Still, the United States was drawn into the war by 1917. That April, the country joined the Allies in fighting against the Central Powers.

Later the same year, future president Herbert Hoover was appointed head of the U.S. Department of Food Administration. The purpose of this wartime agency was to produce and distribute food for both civilian and military needs. This agency is credited with keeping whole nations from starvation. When Hoover called for volunteers to help the millions of European civilians victimized by the conflict, Jane Addams volunteered. Addams applauded the work. But later, in her book *Peace and Bread in Time of War*, she admitted bitterly that if she lived to see another war, she would not open her mouth to say one word about it. She had come to believe that words did no good. "Exhaustion . . . alone can bring a contest of physical force to an end."

By the end of the war in 1918, Jane Addams was securely a public figure, whether she liked it or not. By all indications, she didn't like it. She was never quite at ease as a public speaker and never seemed really comfortable with people outside of those at Hull House. Even people who knew her quite well, said her nephew and biographer James Weber Linn, "felt her love as a radiation rather than as a direct and individual beam. They adored her, but they felt her sometimes to be a little withdrawn." Another friend said, "Despite her affectionate warmth and sympathy and understanding, [there was] something impersonal."

Still others, in her time and afterward, found her humorless. Scholar Jill Conway has written that Addams and the others known as the "great ladies of Chicago" were "high-spirited but not witty, happy but never gay, and curiously one-dimensional. [They were] like characters in a Dickens novel."

A poster from the U.S. Department of Food Administration urges women to conserve food. In 1917, Jane Addams volunteered to work with this agency. Part of that work later involved feeding hungry refugee children. That, as well as her peace activities, would lead some people to view Addams as a traitor to her country.

Be Patriotic
sign your country's
pledge to save the food

U.S. FOOD ADMINISTRATION

War's end

The end of the war brought no slackening in Addams' peace efforts. Although deeply disappointed by her country's failure to join the League of Nations, she continued to work with the government. For most of 1919, she concerned herself with the delivery of food to German and Austrian children. Hunger, she often told people, knows no foes or friends.

She was outraged when Germans living in the Pacific or Africa, who had had no part in the conflict, were thrown out. These innocent people were forced to sell all their property and were then herded into refugee camps where they were not allowed to speak their own language. It reminded her of the Spanish Inquisition in medieval times. Such "blind intolerance . . . does not properly belong to these later centuries," she said. Extreme nationalism — extreme loyalty and devotion to one's nation — was, Addams believed, a great evil. Indeed, such nationalism, with all its distrust masquerading as pride, would be the spur that would drive Germans fueled by anger over their treatment after World War I to try to take over the world not too many years later in World War II. Although even farsighted people such as Jane Addams didn't know it, the next war would be even worse.

All for peace

What Jane Addams did know even then, however, was that peaceful solutions had to be found to avoid such needless suffering. Not long after the war, in 1919, she was elected the first president of the newly formed Women's International League for Peace and Freedom. This organization grew out of the peace conference that had been held in The Hague in 1915.

Soon after her election, Addams, accompanied by Mary Rozet Smith, took a nine-month tour of India, China, Japan, and the Philippines. The intricacy and beauty of India's ancient culture stirred her, but its poverty and illness horribly depressed her. While there, she met Mahatma Gandhi, whose philosophy of action through nonviolent resistance inspired her. In all of these nations far from home, she received a warm reception. She would later write, with a hint of bitterness, that an internationally minded person

"Perhaps nothing is so fraught with significance as the human hand, this oldest tool with which man has dug his way from savagery, and with which he is constantly groping forward."
Jane Addams

"In Jane Addams there are assembled all the best womanly attributes which shall help us to establish peace in the world. . . . She clung to her idealism in the difficult period when other demands and interests overshadowed peace. . . . She was the right spokesman for all the peaceloving women of the world."
Professor Frederick Stang, chairman of the Nobel Committee

should be defined as someone who is seen as a friend to every country except his or her own. Jane Addams' roots in America went deep. Being rejected by her country may have cut even deeper.

And worst of all, Addams knew that the criticism that surrounded her views had cost her beloved Hull House important donations from powerful people. She knew, too, that should her dreams come true and American wealth be distributed more fairly, it would mean the end of the wealthy donors who had helped make so much of her work possible.

But somehow, the budget at Hull House continued to grow, reaching nearly $100,000 a year in the 1920s. The settlement's buildings now covered more than a whole city block. (The original house, which still stands on Halsted Street and is now a museum, was in fact only the smallest part of the whole enterprise.) And through it all, Addams remained strong, guided by her own conscience — her own "inner light." It burned as strongly as ever; she would never disregard its glow. Even four decades after her father's death, Jane Addams was still her father's daughter.

Despite the damage done to Addams' reputation, Hull House survived and continued to grow. Here, the original Hull House building (center of photo) is dwarfed by expansion to either side.

A country unwell

It might be said that throughout the 1920s, Jane Addams felt ashamed and not a little disappointed in her country and its government. Her cheerful optimism, which never denied harsh realities or gave up on changing them, was bruised. It would never entirely heal.

At home in Chicago, Addams saw disturbing signs that the United States was still not on the road back to normal life, as President Warren G. Harding had promised. Rather, Addams thought, it seemed to move forward on a dangerous course, veering between repression and rebellion.

Prohibition came just before the Nineteenth Amendment to the Constitution — the amendment that gave women the vote. Addams was delighted that women finally got the vote, but she wasn't sure about Prohibition, which made it illegal to manufacture or sell alcoholic beverages. Although she did not drink, she didn't begrudge others their habits. As she told a graduating class at Rockford College, her alma mater, "One does good, if at all, with people, not to people. It is easy . . . for us to take liquor away from the . . . immigrant laborer . . . for his good, but the curious result is this — a law passed by people who are quite sure that they themselves do not need the law at all." That was hypocrisy, Addams pointed out, and she had no patience for it.

From bad to worse

But hypocrisy was not the worst of the situation. Addams saw how poor young boys idolized the gangs that secretly continued to produce and distribute liquor. She was saddened by the violence and waste that these "bootleggers" caused trying to provide "hooch." From among these bootleggers came the nation's most infamous gangster, Alphonse ("Al") Capone. He roared out of the West Side of Chicago, where families would flock to gawk at the latest victim of a gangland slaying sprawled on a curb.

Even attitudes within the country were changing. Young people now scorned their parents' European ways and behaved disrespectfully. During her years at Hull House, Addams had watched countless children grow up. Communicating with young people had

"She has a patience which includes all men, all sins, all conditions, all prejudices, all superstitions. Whatever else may be said of her, she is largely tolerant."
Mrs. Elia W. Peattie,
friend of Jane Addams

always been one of her favorite things about her work there. Now even that was growing difficult. People in general seemed less respectful of one another. When the 1924 congress of the Women's International League for Peace and Freedom met in Washington, Addams had to apologize for the way American reporters treated the foreign delegates. Later, when some of the delegates traveled to Chicago, their train had to be diverted. Members of the Ku Klux Klan, the white supremacist organization that had sprung up after the Civil War, were waiting on the depot platform with clubs to threaten the delegates.

The Red Scare

Even worse, to Addams, was the pressure everywhere in American life to shun those whose political or intellectual views differed from those of the majority. Panicky Americans, terrified by stories of the Russian Revolution which had erupted toward the end of World War I, began to look for communists in their midst in what became known as the "Red Scare." Addams called this trend sinister and felt it was probably due to "excessive war propaganda."

She wrote that the prevailing mood "has resulted in a spirit of conformity which has been demanded from all of us in the postwar years on pain of being denounced as a 'Red' or a 'Traitor.'"

Addams herself would become the victim of people's suspicions on several occasions. Certainly that gentle lady who welcomed socialists to her home, championed labor unions, and spoke out for peace might be a communist. "Whose side was Jane Addams on, anyway?" people asked themselves. Addams' name also appeared on a list of fifty-one supposedly dangerous individuals circulated by the Daughters of the American Revolution. Later, members of the American Legion viciously accused her of being pro-German. Even Jane Addams had a limit to her tolerance. "You know," she said, "I am really getting old. I find it is not as easy to love my enemies as it used to be."

In part because she sensed where the stifling of free thought and opinion would lead, Addams helped found the American Civil Liberties Union (ACLU) in 1920. This organization is dedicated to protecting the freedom

Opposite: Carrie Chapman Catt, seen here campaigning, was a major leader in the women's suffrage movement. Although she and Jane Addams disagreed on many issues, the two respected each other's work. When Addams was attacked for her views on peace, Catt defended her, saying, "Miss Addams is one of the greatest women this republic of ours has produced. She has given her life to serve others."

50

The Statue of Liberty was a gift from France honoring the American spirit of freedom. Shortly after World War I, however, people's attitudes seemed to be moving away from the concept of free expression upon which the country had been built. People such as Jane Addams and organizations such as the American Civil Liberties Union helped protect such values.

"She tried to understand those who ignorantly or maliciously misinterpreted her; but rarely did she offer any self-defense. She was almost superhumanly without resentment — even extenuating their abuse as attributable more to prejudice than to evil intent."
    Graham Taylor, friend of
                Jane Addams

of each individual to write, speak, and believe whatever he or she chooses. In its mission, the ACLU has sometimes had to back unpopular causes. At one point, for example, the organization had to defend the right of the hateful American Nazi party, which hated Jews and other minorities, to march through peaceful Jewish neighborhoods. Jane Addams was alive when Adolf Hitler took control of Germany, but she never witnessed the horrors of the Nazis in Europe. It would have saddened her to see Americans embrace even the slogans of such madness. Still, she would have agreed with the ACLU that the cure for evil speech is more speech — of the best, most tolerant kind — not silence enforced by law. Anything else would arouse the ire and suspicion of citizens who believed in democracy.

The Great Depression

The Great Depression hit Chicago like a tornado in 1929. When the New York Stock Exchange collapsed, it did not only signal the end of prosperity for wealthy investors. It also marked the worst period in history for poor Americans. Thousands of people lost their jobs, and when they could not pay rent, lost their homes, too. In "hobo jungles," these now-homeless people warmed their hands at trash fires and helped their children line worn-out shoes with newspaper. People stood in long lines to receive a loaf of bread for their families.

In 1930, with the scourge of the depression still on the land, seventy-year-old Jane Addams watched her struggling neighbors slide even farther into misery. Until Hull House residents reached out and showed them how to get it, many immigrants did not even understand that there was such a thing as public relief. Others were too proud to ask. Addams believed that principles of working together were even more urgent. "Unless normal times return soon," she predicted, "the United States will be faced with the strange problem of taking care of a demoralized generation."

The second volume of her autobiography, called *The Second Twenty Years at Hull House*, was published that same year. It reflected Addams' unwavering commitment to settlement work. And it proved, to her satisfaction, that educated young women could venture out even into the most dismal, dangerous slums and make real changes for good in the lives of those they found there. She, as a member of the first generation of American women to attend college, was particularly proud of that point.

The book and her work at Hull House had promoted this belief. Through Hull House, many well-to-do young people had learned to put the grand ideas of their education into practice. They had learned to "express the meaning of life in terms of life itself, in forms of activity." But not all of the Hull House residents were young women of the privileged class. Plenty of young men worked there as well, including: John Dewey, the educational philosopher; Gerard Swope, who became president of General Electric Company; and William Lyon Mackenzie King, who became the prime minister of Canada. Photographer Wallace Kirkland, whose

"In time we came to define a settlement as an institution attempting to learn from life itself."
Jane Addams

impressive pictures in *Life* magazine won him great acclaim, lived at Hull House for fifteen years, teaching neighborhood boys how to use cameras. "We always thought of Jane Addams as a lovable grandmother, never as an old maid or a social worker," he recalled.

A Nobel Prize winner

But in spite of such loving friends, Addams' reputation continued to suffer in many circles. Some people refused to let her forget how much they detested her pacifist principles. But during this very bleak time, Jane Addams received what many people consider her most shining achievement: the Nobel Peace Prize. She was awarded the prize on December 10, 1931. She shared the honor with Nicholas Murray Butler, the president of Columbia University, who won for his work with the Carnegie Endowment for International Peace. To Addams, the award justified her pacifist work to the world.

Unfortunately, Addams could not travel to Norway to accept her award. On the day of the ceremony, she was awaiting surgery in a Baltimore hospital. There, she could only read what Frederick Stang, of the Nobel Committee in Norway, said of her: "She clung to her idealism in the difficult period when other demands and interests overshadowed peace."

By 1932, Addams seemed well on her way to being reinstated as a national hero. During these final years of her life, she was honored as no American woman had been honored before, receiving fourteen honorary degrees. One of these degrees came from Yale; it was the first honorary degree the school had ever given to a woman. And in the presidential election of 1932, both Republicans and Democrats invited Jane Addams to present her views to their platform committees. This marked a magnificent achievement for any woman of the time, much less such a controversial woman.

When election time came, Addams voted for her old friend, Herbert Hoover. But the people were demanding more drastic solutions than Hoover, a Republican, offered. They turned, instead, to Democrat Franklin D. Roosevelt and his "New Deal" for social welfare. Roosevelt swept into office on a high tide of public support. Jane Addams liked what Roosevelt

Alfred Nobel established the Nobel Prizes with the fortune he earned from his invention of dynamite. These prizes are awarded each year to people whose work is judged as having the "greatest benefit on mankind." Categories for the prizes include economics, chemistry, literature, peace, physics, and physiology or medicine.

had to say. He saw the need to wage peaceful war, as he said, "against the inequalities and resentments" that he feared would breed revolution in America.

Life goes on

As always, life went on at Hull House. In 1932, the critic and writer Edmund Wilson visited the settlement. While there, he observed the effects of the Great Depression, noting that it had deepened the misery in the neighborhood and that "unemployment and want — terrifying specters at the best of times — were now more demoralizing than ever."

"They say," Wilson continued, "that Jane Addams always had a sad face, even before she became a professional neighbor and a conscious patriot. Certainly her face is sad now." But he added that Addams had not lost her courage and patience.

Wilson also wrote that Hull House had always stood for tolerance: "All the parties and all the faiths had found asylum there." It was still so, but even though Addams preached acceptance of people as they were, she never fully accepted that idea herself. Instead, Addams always looked for people's higher natures. She always hoped for a little more. In her own words, she defined her political philosophy as hoping for the "best possible."

The final days

Jane Addams had not been well for many years, and she suffered a heart attack not long after her seventieth birthday. But not even that was the final blow to the frail constitution that had carried the sickly little girl from Cedarville so far for so long. The endless round of public appearances took up much of her time, but she went willingly. Although friends said she was "always trying to be inconspicuous," Jane Addams never liked to miss a chance to advance her cause. A doctor friend said of Addams, "She will have to wear herself out. She can't rust out; it isn't her way."

In May 1935, only a matter of days following a last public meeting, Jane Addams suffered a severe pain in her left side. An operation revealed cancer so severe that doctors were afraid she would never regain consciousness. She did.

Franklin D. Roosevelt and running mate John Nance Garner (above) won the 1932 election by a landslide. Although Jane Addams liked Roosevelt's ideas, she had supported her friend Herbert Hoover in the election. Addams soon became a loyal supporter of the new administration.

Jane Addams died on May 21, 1935. Here, a smattering of the thousands of mourners who attended the funeral crowd a corner of the Hull House courtyard.

"When I was a child," she told friends at her bedside, "an old doctor friend . . . told me that the hardest thing in the world to kill was an old woman. He seems to have been right."

On May 21, 1935, Jane Addams died.

After she lay in state at Hull House, a hearse carried her body to the railroad station to be shipped home to Cedarville. As the vehicle came to the corner of Halsted and Twelfth streets, a police officer directing traffic asked the driver, "Is it she?"

"It is," the driver replied.

"She goes in peace," the officer said softly. Holding up his hand, he stopped the traffic until long after the car had made the turn and gone on its way.

Jane Addams remembered

Illinois governor Henry Horner said, in tribute to Jane Addams, "I think of her as of the evening star, drawing the imagination of man through the clouds to the knowledge of a light that cannot fail."

Frances Perkins, Roosevelt's secretary of labor and the first woman cabinet officer in U.S. history, made a more practical tribute, the kind Jane Addams, who was absolutely unmoved by flattery, might have liked: "[She] really invented social work and social welfare as a department of life in the United States."

Jane Addams was buried in Cedarville near the father who had been the all of her life. Her plain tombstone has no dates. Only these words mark the site: "Jane Addams of Hull House and the Women's International League for Peace and Freedom." These are honest words. She had devoted friends and enthusiastic admirers. But for the half century that she lived after her father died, Jane Addams had little personal life as such.

But personal life or no, she did more than "inhabit reality." She became her work. She gave herself so wholly to her mission that it satisfied the needs for the love of a family that other women might have missed. And as the feminists of the latter half of the twentieth century say, the personal is political. This equation was never truer for anyone than for Jane Addams.

Her mark on the world

Just before she died, on May 2, 1935, Jane Addams was in Washington for the twentieth anniversary of the Women's International League for Peace and Freedom.

"[Her closest associates] sometimes felt her love as a radiation rather than as a direct and individual beam. They adored her, but they felt her sometimes to be a little withdrawn."

James Weber Linn, Jane Addams' nephew

Just before her death in 1935, Jane Addams chats with reporters at the twentieth-anniversary celebration of the Women's International League for Peace and Freedom. By this time, Addams was once again recognized as one of the great women of her time.

"I sat here wondering what kind of person I was that you should be seeing not me, but this mirage you have described. I assure you it is not there. I am a very simple person."
Jane Addams

Among the countless tributes given her that day, one stood out. It came from First Lady Eleanor Roosevelt. That night, Roosevelt said, "It is for being yourself that I thank you tonight. When the day comes when difficulties are faced and settled without resorting to the type of waste which war has always meant, we shall look back in this country upon the leadership you have given us, Miss Addams."

Frail and obviously ill, Jane Addams rose slowly to the podium when it was her turn to speak. She glanced at her script, then put it down. She would not use it that night. What she said next turned out to be her final advice to the world: "Nothing could be worse than the fear that one had given up too soon, and had left one effort unexpended which might have saved the world."

Jane Addams did not save the world, but she saved many small parts of it, on the streets of Chicago and in the refugee villages of Europe. And her efforts — through her words and lessons, but mainly through the young people whose lives she touched — insure her immortality.

And through it all, she never, not once, gave up.

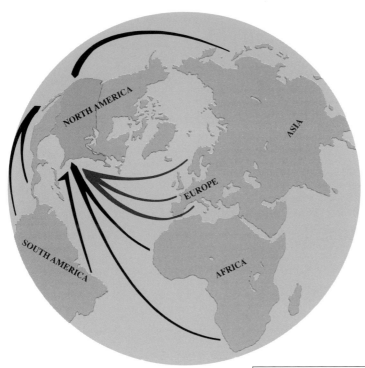

| | Immigration to the United States, 1890s-1920s |
| | Immigration to the United States, 1930s-1980s |

For More Information . . .

Organizations

If you would like to know more about Jane Addams or want to get in touch with groups which are carrying on her work in some way, write to the organizations listed below. When you write, be sure to be specific about what you want to know and always remember to include your full name, your age, and your return address.

American Civil Liberties Union (ACLU)
132 West 43rd Street
New York, NY 10036

Jane Addams-Hull House Museum
University of Illinois at Chicago
Chicago, IL 60680

Women's International League for
    Peace and Freedom
1213 Race Street
Philadelphia, PA 19107

Jane Addams Peace Association
777 United Nations Plaza
New York, NY 10017

National Association for the
Advancement of Colored People(NAACP)
4805 Mt. Hope Drive
Baltimore, MD 21215

The Peace Museum
430 West Erie Street
Chicago, IL 60610

Books

About Jane Addams —

Dreams Into Deeds: Nine Women Who Dared. Linda Peavy and Ursula Smith
    (Macmillan)
Jane Addams: Social Reformer Feminist. Jane Horde (Facts on File)
Jane Addams. Cynthia Klindel and Dan Zadra (Creative Education)
Jane Addams of Hull-House. Winifred Esther Wise (Harcourt, Brace and Co.)
Jane Addams: Social Worker. Mary Kittredge (Chelsea House)
The Value of Friendship: The Story of Jane Addams. Ann D. Johnson (Oak Tree)

About Peace —

Challenge of Peace. Mulford Sibley and Marjorie Sibley (Dillon)
Learning Peace. Grace Abrams and Fran Schmidt (Jane Addams Peace Association)
Now About Peace. James McKinnell (Brethren Press)
The Peace Seekers: The Nobel Peace Prize. Nathan Aaseng (Lerner)
A Peaceable Warrior. Marguerite Murray (Macmillan)
Peacemakers: Informing the World. Jane North (Dillon)

Further Reading —

The following titles, which will probably appeal more to older readers, also contain
valuable and interesting information about Jane Addams and her work. Two of the titles,
in fact, were written by Addams.

American Heroine: The Life and Legend of Jane Addams. Allen F. Davis (Oxford)
Illustrious Americans: Jane Addams. Marshall W. Fishwick (Silver Burdett Co.)
Jane Addams: A Biography. James Weber Linn (D. Appleton Century Co.)
The Second Twenty Years at Hull House. Jane Addams (Macmillan)
Twenty Years at Hull House. Jane Addams (Signet Classics)

Glossary

American Civil Liberties Union (ACLU)
    An organization founded by Jane Addams, Helen Keller, Eugene V. Debs, and others
    in 1920 to protect the freedoms guaranteed in the Bill of Rights. The ACLU offers
    legal aid to people whose civil rights are endangered. Among the causes it supports
    are freedom of speech, freedom of religion, and freedom from discrimination.

anarchists
    People who believe that all forms of government restrict personal freedom and
    should be abolished.

cholera
    A disease caused by drinking contaminated water. Cholera is a very dangerous
    disease, both because it spreads rapidly to become an epidemic and because people
    who catch it often die before they can get help.

Daughters of the American Revolution (DAR)
An organization founded in 1890, made up of women descended from men who fought in the American Revolution. Originally a liberal organization that supported child labor laws, consumer protection, and other progressive legislation, it became extremely conservative during World War I.

Dewey, John (1859-1952)
U.S. educator, philosopher, and psychologist. As a teacher, Dewey sought to reform American schools by putting the emphasis on the student rather than the subject taught. He was a lifelong friend and supporter of Jane Addams and Hull House.

immigrants
People who leave their own country to begin a new life in another.

James, William (1842-1910)
Psychologist and philosopher, brother to novelist Henry James. His school of thought, called pragmatism, emphasized the practical results of ideas. He was a good friend and influence on John Dewey and a supporter of Hull House.

Ku Klux Klan (KKK)
A terrorist organization founded by white racists just after the Civil War. Its goal was to use threats and violence to prevent African-Americans from gaining the rights granted them by the Thirteenth, Fourteenth, and Fifteenth amendments. Outlawed by President Ulysses S. Grant, it disbanded in 1871 but sprang up again forty years later as an anti-Catholic, anti-Jewish, antiforeign group. It vanished again during the Great Depression but returned a third time in the 1950s and 1960s as an anti-civil-rights group.

League of Nations
An international organization founded by Woodrow Wilson in 1919 to promote international cooperation and prevent the outbreak of war by offering diplomatic means for nations to resolve their disagreements. The United States refused to join the league after World War I ended, which badly undercut the league's authority and its power to resolve world crises. Very successful in the 1920s, it declined in the 1930s and was replaced in 1945 by the United Nations.

Nobel Prize
A series of prizes founded by Alfred Nobel, the inventor of dynamite. Each year, prizes are awarded in the fields of chemistry, economics, literature, peace, physics, and physiology or medicine to the person or persons judged to have made the greatest contribution to humankind.

pacifism
The belief that violence and war are wrong. People who are pacifists object to these as methods of settling disagreements and refuse to take another human life, even in self-defense.

Quakers
Members of the Society of Friends, a branch of Christianity. Quakers believe in following individual consciences rather than any outside authority. They are also well known for their tolerance and pacifism.

Roosevelt, Theodore (1858-1919)
The youngest person ever to become president of the United States. A liberal reformer, he supported many laws regulating big business, setting aside land for national parks, and placing quality controls on food and medicines.

Ruskin, John (1819-1900)
English art critic, social critic, and author. He not only defended unorthodox painters such as John Turner and Dante Gabriel Rossetti, but he also criticized the Victorian Era and Industrial Revolution for destroying both natural beauty and people's sense of humanity. Among his most famous books are *The Stones of Venice* and *Seven Lamps of Architecture*.

Starr, Ellen Gates (1859-1940)
Cofounder of Hull House and friend of Jane Addams. Starr was both more radical than Addams in her commitment to the labor movement and other reform issues and more interested in bringing culture to the poor of Chicago's slums. Late in life she converted to Catholicism and became a nun shortly before her death.

suffrage
The right to vote. The suffrage movement was the crusade to grant women the right to vote in all elections. After decades of struggle, American women won this right through the ratification of the Nineteenth Amendment in 1920.

sweatshops
Factories that exploit workers, especially immigrants, by making them work long hours under harsh conditions at low wages.

Tolstoy, Leo (1828-1910)
Russian novelist, author of *War and Peace* and *Anna Karenina*, who argued that one should live simply. Although he was born a wealthy nobleman, Tolstoy lived like a poor farmer and eventually gave up all his possessions. He also became a devout Christian and pacifist. At the time Addams visited him, he was considered the world's greatest living author.

Toynbee Hall
An early experiment in the settlement movement and the inspiration for Hull House. This London building provided a chance for university men to live in working-class neighborhoods and share their culture with their slum neighbors. Their goal, like that of Hull House, was to make fine art, music, and literature available to poor people and to break down social and economic barriers.

typhoid fever
A disease contracted by drinking contaminated water. Before the days of modern medicine, it often caused epidemics in which hundreds were killed. About one-third of all the people who caught the disease died of it.

Chronology

1860   **September 6** — Jane Addams is born in Cedarville, Illinois, the youngest of five surviving children of John and Sarah Addams.
November — Abraham Lincoln is elected president.

1861	**April**— The U.S. Civil War begins. Addams' father organizes and finances a troop of Union soldiers.
1863	**January** — Sarah Addams has a miscarriage and dies.
1865	**April** — Abraham Lincoln is assassinated.
1866	Martha Addams dies suddenly of typhoid fever.
1868	John Addams marries Anna Haldeman. Mary Addams marries John Linn.
1871	The Great Chicago Fire destroys most of the city. The fifteen-year-old Charles J. Hull mansion is one of the few houses to survive.
1876	Alice Addams marries her stepbrother, Harry Haldeman.
1877	Jane Addams begins study at Rockford Seminary, where she meets Ellen Gates Starr.
1881	Addams graduates from Rockford Seminary. Addams becomes ill and abandons her plans to attend Smith College in the fall. **July 2** — President James A. Garfield is shot. **August** — John Addams dies suddenly of appendicitis. **September 19** — President Garfield dies. Jane and Anna Addams move to Philadelphia, where Jane briefly attends the Women's Medical College of Philadelphia.
1882	**February** — Addams leaves the Women's Medical College of Philadelphia because of ill health. She spends the next two months taking a rest cure. Addams undergoes major surgery on her back to correct a curvature of her spine.
1883	Weber Addams suffers a nervous breakdown. Jane Addams begins managing the family's properties and finances. **August** — Addams leaves for a two-year tour of Europe with her stepmother and Sarah Anderson, a teacher she had befriended at Rockford.
1885	Addams returns home, suffering from depression and a sense of purposelessness. She moves to Baltimore with her stepmother, where she begins visiting charitable institutions and learning about the work done there.
1886	The Haymarket Riot between police strikebreakers and union supporters leaves seven men dead in Chicago.
1887	Addams accepts a temporary teaching post at Rockford College (formerly Rockford Seminary). She quits after one day. **December** — Addams travels to Europe again, accompanied by Ellen Gates Starr and Sarah Anderson.
1888	**June** — Addams and Starr visit Toynbee Hall in London. **October** — Addams joins the Presbyterian church and decides to become a lay missionary to the poor.

1889	**January** — Addams moves to Chicago to live with Starr. They plan their own version of Toynbee Hall somewhere in Chicago. **September** — Addams and Starr move into Hull House.

1889   **January** — Addams moves to Chicago to live with Starr. They plan their own version of Toynbee Hall somewhere in Chicago.
                    September — Addams and Starr move into Hull House.

1892   Florence Kelley of Hull House is appointed by the state of Illinois to investigate mistreatment of immigrant workers in sweatshops. Her report leads to new laws the next year designed to protect women and children working in factories.
John Dewey visits Hull House for the first time and becomes both a friend of Addams and a loyal supporter of Hull House.

1893   Addams becomes popular as a speaker and guest lecturer. Reporters start to call her "Saint Jane."

1894   Addams' eldest sister, Mary Linn, dies. Addams becomes guardian of her nephew Stanley Linn.

1895   Addams becomes garbage inspector for the Nineteenth Ward.

1895-
1898   Hull House fights Chicago alderman Johnny Powers in an attempt to end corruption and improve conditions in the Nineteenth Ward.

1896   Addams suffers from typhoid fever. She travels to Europe to recover her strength. She meets Leo Tolstoy.

1898   Addams publishes "The College Woman and the Family Claim," about how difficult it is for women to gain independence from their families.
The Spanish-American War breaks out. Addams becomes involved in the peace movement.

1899   The country's first juvenile court is established in Illinois.

1901   President William McKinley is shot by Leon Czolgosz and dies eight days later. Theodore Roosevelt becomes president.

1902   Addams' first book, *Democracy and Social Ethics*, is published.

1904   The University of Wisconsin gives Addams the first of her many honorary degrees.

1905   Addams is appointed to the Chicago school board and tries to carry out reforms affecting education.

1906   A magazine article hails Addams as "The Only Saint America Has Produced."

1907   Addams publishes *Newer Ideals for Peace*, her second book. It is attacked by Roosevelt as "naive."
Addams becomes involved with the women's suffrage movement and chairs Chicago's Committee for Municipal Suffrage for Women.

1909   The National Association for the Advancement of Colored People (NAACP) is founded with Addams' support. She becomes a member of its executive committee.
Addams publishes *The Spirit of Youth and the City Streets*, about the

problems of juvenile delinquents.
Addams also becomes the first woman to receive an honorary degree from Yale.

1910   Addams publishes her autobiography, *Twenty Years at Hull House.*

1912   Addams campaigns in support of former president Theodore Roosevelt's Progressive ("Bull Moose") party.
Addams publishes a book about prostitution, *A New Conscience and an Ancient Evil.*

1913   Chicago grants women the vote in all local elections.

1914   World War I begins. The United States remains neutral.

1915   **January** — The Woman's Peace party is founded, with Addams as chairperson.
April — Addams and forty others sail to Holland to attend an international women's peace conference, joining one thousand other delegates from twelve countries.
May-June — Addams visits London, Berlin, Vienna, Budapest, Rome, Bern, and Paris, carrying the conference's propeace message to the leaders of both sides of warring countries.
July — Addams returns to the United States, where she is attacked for her antiwar activities.
December — Addams falls gravely ill with kidney trouble, from which she never fully recovers.

1917   **April** — The United States enters the war. Addams is one of the few antiwar activists to continue her efforts for peace.

1918   Addams begins working with Secretary of Commerce Herbert Hoover's Food Administration to help feed European allies.
November 11 — World War I ends.

1919   **April** — Addams visits Paris and sees the battle sites on the Western Front. She attends a women's conference in Zurich and is elected president of the newly founded Women's International League for Peace and Freedom.
July — Addams visits Berlin and is appalled by the starving children there. She works to have food sent to the defeated countries, setting off a fresh wave of criticism.

1919-1920   The Red Scare: thousands of people are arrested on charges of being Communist spies. Hundreds are deported, and new laws are passed preventing people from immigrating to America.

1920   **January** — Prohibition begins.
August — The Nineteenth Amendment is ratified, granting women the right to vote in all elections.
November — Warren G. Harding is elected president and promises to pursue a policy of isolation. He begins suspending or curtailing many of the reforms of the preceding twenty years.

Addams helps found the American Civil Liberties Union in response to the Red Scare.

1922 Addams publishes *Peace and Bread in Time of War*, recounting her wartime activities to help feed the people of Europe. She undertakes a nine-month trip to the Orient, visiting India, Burma, the Philippines, China, and Japan. She undergoes emergency cancer surgery in Tokyo.

1924 Delegates to the annual meeting of the Women's International League for Peace and Freedom in Washington are denounced as spies and foreigners by the DAR and American Legion.

1926 Addams suffers a heart attack and has to cut back on her activities as her health fails.

1928 Addams' old friend Herbert Hoover is elected president, predicting an end to poverty and promising an era of prosperity.

1929 Addams resigns as head of the Women's International League for Peace and Freedom because of poor health.
October — The New York Stock Exchange collapses, marking the beginning of the Great Depression.

1930 Addams publishes *The Second Twenty Years at Hull House,* a continuation of her autobiography.
Addams suffers another heart attack.

1931 Addams is awarded the Nobel Peace Prize.
Addams undergoes surgery for a tumor.

1932 Franklin D. Roosevelt is elected president. His New Deal policies include most of the reforms Addams had been fighting for for over forty years.

1934 Mary Rozet Smith dies.

1935 **May 21** — Jane Addams dies of cancer.

Index